Copyright © Jordan Johnson

All rights reserved

No part of this publication may be reproduced or distributed in any form or by any means, electronic or mechanical, or stored in a database or retrieval system, without prior written permission from the author/publisher.

The author/owner claims no responsibility to any person or entity for any liability, loss, or damage caused or alleged to be caused by directly or indirectly as a result of the use, application, or interpretation of the information presented herein.

Cover cow photo and photography on pages 7, 10, 11, 25 (top picture) by Tyra Nishell.
Full size cover photo, food photography, and all others by Marlen Beezley.

Contents

Foreword... 3
Spoonfuls Matter... 5
Why Beef?... 7
What To Expect... 8
Sourcing Beef... 10
Sourcing Produce... 12
Recipes... 14
References... 23
Meat The Maker... 24

Foreword

When I was a first-time mom I wanted to do everything right for our newborn daughter, Scarlett. When it was time for her to start eating food I read all of the books and the blogs, asked the experts, and talked to seasoned moms about where and how to start, but I still felt confused. My instincts were telling me that she needed high-nutrition foods like the meat and eggs that benefited me as an adult, but every baby expert out there seemed to only focus on purees made with fruits and vegetables.

I trusted my gut and my daughter's first food was a beef puree. To my surprise, she loved it! Looking back now, my only wish is that I had been able to read this type of cook book when I first got started on my journey as a mother.

Jordan has created a masterpiece that puts to rest misconceptions about meat as a food for infants, while making it totally easy to prepare foods that are appropriate for infants at every stage.

- Amanda Radke, Mother of Four
Bachelors of Science, Agricultural Communication, Education & Leadership

"Little mouths turn into adult appetites."

We can't expect our five year-old children to eat a plate full of meat and vegetables if their infant palates have been overloaded with fruit purees and corn puffs from the beginning. The very first foods to saturate their tongue play a major role in palatability and food preferences for the rest of their life.

These beefy first foods are simple to prepare, will expand your baby's palette, adjust their taste buds for nourishing whole foods, and aid in their growth and development for years to come. The food you serve has a purpose in fueling and nourishing your baby's little body. You are not simply filling their stomach with substance; this is so much bigger!

Spoonfuls Matter

Your baby uses his muscles and energy to become more mobile; imagine rolling over, crawling, and eventually the days of walking and running. As she continuously tests the cause and effects of trial and error. As he takes in new surroundings, colors, shapes, sounds, smells, and tastes. As she works through every major, new emotion.

All these physical, emotional, and mental responses require nutrients, minerals, protein, and fats to generate and distribute energy. You are about to fuel your little one's energy stores with one of the most nutrient dense foods available on the planet!

Why Beef?

Choosing beef is an affordable, efficient, natural, and nourishing source of food. It is a high source of protein, vitamin B6 and B12, choline, phosphorus, iron, selenium, zinc, and other essential minerals and vitamins. All of which support a growing infant with brain development, immune function, organ function, energy, red blood cell health, oxygen transportation, and so much more.

Essential nutrients such as choline and vitamin b6 support the brain and nervous system, aids in memory, mood regulation, and muscle control. Phosphorus supports the formation of bones and teeth. Iron supports energy and focus. It is a key mineral in carrying oxygen to the muscles.

Zinc and selenium support the immune system by helping fight off viruses. Protein is essential for building and repairing the body's tissues and systems.

Vitamin B12 regulates your nervous system, establishes healthy blood cells, and generates DNA. Did you know animal products are the only way to naturally source vitamin B12? You cannot get this essential nutrient naturally elsewhere; beef being one of the highest available forms of this vitamin.

All of these essential nutrients are found in high values in just one single serving of beef. It is one of the most nutrient dense and protein packed foods available.

What To Expect

All you need is a blender or food processor to mix together these ingredients. The recipes are meant to be bountiful with beef and convenient. While the consistency of each baby food recipe doesn't always appear appetizing, I assure you that it tastes wonderful! These recipes have been taste-tested and approved by mama, daddy, and baby. Our motto in the kitchen is delicious and nutritious! You will find in the cooking directions the consistency is going to differ from a fruit or veggie liquid puree. The consistency is slightly thicker and is intended to be this way.

Whether you are a first-time parent or have a houseful of blessings already, my hope is that you not only feel comfortable but feel confident feeding your infant beef. This is greater than preparing a "high protein meal" for your baby. This is about creating a palate for whole, natural foods and increasing their likeliness of having a well-rounded diet from infancy through adulthood.

When I see my daughter's eyes spark with creativity, when I see her excitement for food, when I see her explore each meal, when I see her actively thinking and making decisions, I know that her beef-based diet plays a substantial role in her awareness and mindfulness. I have watched her time and time again regularly choose beef over mac and cheese or decline a sweet chocolate treat when offered.

> *"Cooking is a creative science"*

Prepared in a timely manner with convenience and armed with all the nutritional benefits. Mamas, daddies, and caregivers will be able to confidently incorporate beef as one of your baby's very first foods. I am so proud of you! Preparing these recipes should be fun (don't forget that!). Cooking is a creative science and I hope you enjoy these formulations.

This book is for anyone feeding a little one. Whether you are raising cattle yourself or live in an apartment complex in one of the largest cities in the country. I pray you are encouraged, inspired, and empowered with these beefy recipes.

Sourcing Beef

Really quick! I want you to know this from the depths of my mothering heart. No matter whether you buy your ingredients fresh at the farmers market, off the store's shelves, grow your own produce, or buy them in a tin can, I am proud of you for taking the extra step to learn, grow, and prepare beef dishes for your precious angel.

Buying beef directly from the rancher ensures knowing where your meat comes from and provides the opportunity to ask important questions. There is full transparency in animal practices throughout the operation, including veterinary care, nutrition programs, and stress management strategies.

It is more affordable to buy beef directly from the rancher, in comparison to the store. Cha-ching! You are bypassing the middleman which cuts down on facility, transportation, and processing costs. You can buy beef in bulk from the rancher by purchasing a ¼ or ½ of a cow or you can buy beef in cuts, such as pounds of ground beef.

If you cannot connect with a rancher or are unsure of where to buy local beef, you still have options! You can purchase from a local butcher shop, farmers market, or a co-op. The great thing about shopping at a co-op is the grocery store will source local meat first to fill their shelves. You have a high chance of purchasing beef raised humanely and local to you within the convenience of shopping at a supermarket.

"From the ground up. Beef and babies."

Sourcing Produce

When you buy produce *in season* they are picked at their peak ripeness. This means your baby gets a better tasting and nutrient dense crop. Don't forget to buy at your community farmer's market or stop at one of those delightful roadside produce stands to buy your fruits and vegetables.

"Beef Giving" is a great winter recipe for this reason. Whereas "Blue-Beary" is a wonderful late summer recipe. Fortunately, living in a modern society, we all have access to grocery stores that offer an abundance of produce continuously, making these recipes easy to source throughout the year.

Blue-Beary

This recipe gets a special spotlight as our very first, beef baby food ever made. It's also where our daughter was dubbed her nickname "bear" for loving this recipe so much.

Yields 10 oz

Ingredients
1 cup ground beef
1 cup blueberries (Fresh produce will yield higher nutrients and minerals, but you can always use frozen!)
Water

Directions
Add ¼ cup of water and ground beef to the skillet. Cook at a low-medium temperature until it is well done.

Add beef and blueberries to food processor. Blend until the consistency is a thick puree.

You may add more water to get a consistency you are comfortable with. Start with 1 tbsp at a time.

Storage
Store in food pouches or glass jars. Recipe is good for up to 3 months in the freezer. If storing in the fridge, use within 3-4 days.

Beef Giving

Yields 10 oz

Ingredients
1 cup ground beef
½ cup sweet potato (small sweet potato)
¼ cup cooked cranberries
Water

Directions
Add ¼ cup of water and ground beef to the skillet. Cook at a low-medium temperature until it is well done.
Peel sweet potato and cut into 1 inch squares. Add potato to pot of water and boil for 25 minutes.
They should be soft when poked with a fork.

While the potatoes are cooking, cover cranberries with water in a separate pot and bring to a boil. Reduce heat to medium and simmer for 15 minutes. Then strain both pots.

Add sweet potato, ground beef, and cranberry to the blender. Blend until the consistency is a thick puree. You may add more water to get a consistency you are comfortable with. Start with 1 tbsp at a time.

Storage
Store in food pouches or glass jars. Recipe is good for up to 3 months in the freezer. If storing in the fridge, use within 3-4 days.

The Carrot On Top

Yields 15 oz

Ingredients
1 cup ground beef
2 small long-stem carrots
2 apricots (May use canned when fresh is not available. Look for fruit canned in water. If only "in syrup" is available, be sure to rinse the fruit well.)
Water

Directions
Add ¼ cup of water and ground beef to the skillet. Cook at a low-medium temperature until it is well done.
Cut long stem carrots in half.

Covering the carrots with water in a pot, bring to a boil. Reduce heat and simmer for 20-25 minutes, or until carrots are tender. Then strain.

Add ground beef, carrot, and pitted apricot to the food processor. Blend until the consistency is a thick puree. You may add more water to get a consistency you are comfortable with. Start with 1 tbsp at a time.

Storage
Store in food pouches or glass jars. Recipe is good for up to 3 months in the freezer. If storing in the fridge, use within 3-4 days.

Fiesta

Yields 14 oz

Ingredients
1 cup ground beef
½ of an avocado
¼ of cilantro bunch
Water

Directions
Add ¼ cup of water and ground beef to he skillet. Cook at a low-medium temperature until it is well done. Cut avocado in half and remove seed and rind. Finely chop up cilantro. Add ground beef, cilantro, and avocado to food processor. Blend until the consistency is a thick puree. You may add more water to get a consistency you are comfortable with. Start with 1 tbsp at a time.

Storage
Store in food pouches or glass jars. Recipe is good for up to 3 months in the freezer. If storing in the fridge, use within 3-4 days.

Classic Beef Stew

Yields 12 oz

Ingredients
1 small long-stem carrot
2 small yellow potatoes
¼ cup peas
¾ cup beef
Water
Pinch of onion powder

Directions
Add ¼ cup of water and ground beef to the skillet. Cook at a low-medium temperature until it is well done. Add potatoes and carrot to pot and boil for 20 minutes. They should be soft when poked with a fork. After 20 minutes add peas to the pot and boil all together for an additional 5 minutes. Then strain.
Add the beef, carrots, potatoes, a pinch of onion powder, and water to food processor. Blend until the consistency is a thick puree. You may add more water to get a consistency you are comfortable with. Start with 1 tbsp at a time.

Storage
Store in food pouches or glass jars. Recipe is good for up to 3 months in the freezer. If storing in the fridge, use within 3-4 days.

Can't Beet It

Yields 14 oz

Ingredients
1 cup ground beef
2 small beets or 3/4 cup beet
3 mint leaves
Water

Directions
Add ¼ cup of water and ground beef to the skillet. Cook at a low-medium temperature until it is well done.
Finely chop up mint leaves.
If using fresh beets - cover the beets with water in a pot and boil for 30-45 minutes.
Let beets cool slightly, peel the skin off while still warm, then cut into 1 inch squares.

Add ground beef, mint, and water to food processor.
Blend until the consistency is a thick puree.
You may add more water to get a consistency you are comfortable with. Start with 1 tbsp at a time.

Storage
Store in food pouches or glass jars.
Recipe is good for up to 3 months in the freezer. If storing in the fridge,
use within 3-4 days.

So Gourd For You

Yields 12 oz

Ingredients
1 cup ground beef
3/4 cup pumpkin
1/4 tsp cinnamon
Water

Note* I recommend using a fresh sugar/pie pumpkin (these are the cute, small pumpkins at the store or patch). However, you can use 100% pure puree pumpkin from the can.

Directions
If using a fresh pumpkin, preheat oven to 350 degrees F (176 C).
Cut the pumpkin in half from top to bottom.
Scrape out the seeds and strings with a spoon.
Brush the inside of each pumpkin half with a light coat of butter.
Lay both pumpkin halves face down on a baking sheet.
Bake pumpkin at 350 degrees F for 45-60 minutes.
Peel off the pumpkin skin. This is easiest when the pumpkins are still warm but have not cooled down completely.

While your pumpkin is baking, add ¼ cup of water and ground beef to the skillet. Cook at a low-medium temperature until it is well done.

Add the ground beef, pumpkin, and cinnamon to food processor. Blend until the consistency is a thick puree. You may add more water to get a consistency you are comfortable with. Start with 1 tbsp at a time.

Storage
Store in food pouches or glass jars. Recipe is good for up to 3 months in the freezer. If storing in the fridge, use within 3-4 days.

Breakfast Beef

Yields 8 oz

Ingredients
¾ cup beef
2 scrambled eggs
¼ cup mushrooms
Water

Directions
Add ¼ cup of water and ground beef to skillet. Cook at a low-medium temperature until it is well done. Scramble two eggs in skillet.

Add cut mushrooms, beef, and scrambled eggs to food processor. Blend until consistency is a thick puree. You may add more water to get a consistency you are comfortable with. Start with 1 tbsp at a time.

Storage
Store in food pouches or glass jars. Recipe is good for up to 3 months in the freezer. If storing in the fridge, use within 3-4 days.

References

U.S. Department of Health and Human Services. (n.d.). *Vitamin and mineral supplement fact sheet*. NIH Office of Dietary Supplements. Retrieved January 2, 2022, from https://ods.od.nih.gov/factsheets/list-VitaminsMinerals/

Sunde RA. Selenium. In: Ross AC, Caballero B, Cousins RJ, Tucker KL, Ziegler TR, eds. Modern Nutrition in Health and Disease. 11th ed. Philadelphia, PA: Lippincott Williams & Wilkins; 2012:225-37 (https://ods.od.nih.gov/factsheets/Selenium-HealthProfessional/#en1) U.S. Department of Agriculture, Agricultural Research Service. 2013. USDA National Nutrient Database for Standard Reference, Release 26. Available at: http://www.ars.usda.gov/ba/bhnrc/ndl.

Meat The Maker

I didn't grow up around cows, horses, or any part of agriculture, but have been drawn to the western lifestyle for as long as I can remember. Here I am now, a first-generation cattle producer, registered nurse, wife, and mother. I have one baby that is currently cooking in the oven and a toddler who fully inspired this entire book! At just five-months-old our daughter had her very first food... you guessed it! Beef.

People thought we were crazy for not following the traditional baby food route, but if you ask me this is as primal as it gets! I knew the kind of food I fed my baby was important, so I mixed some beef and berries together. After that I couldn't stop talking about beef based baby food.

"We can best serve our families and bodies in two places, the kitchen and the outdoors."

Made in the USA
Middletown, DE
13 July 2024